AF226000

ANDY LEBLANC

Sleepytime Tales

Mindful Bedtime Stories for Restful Nights

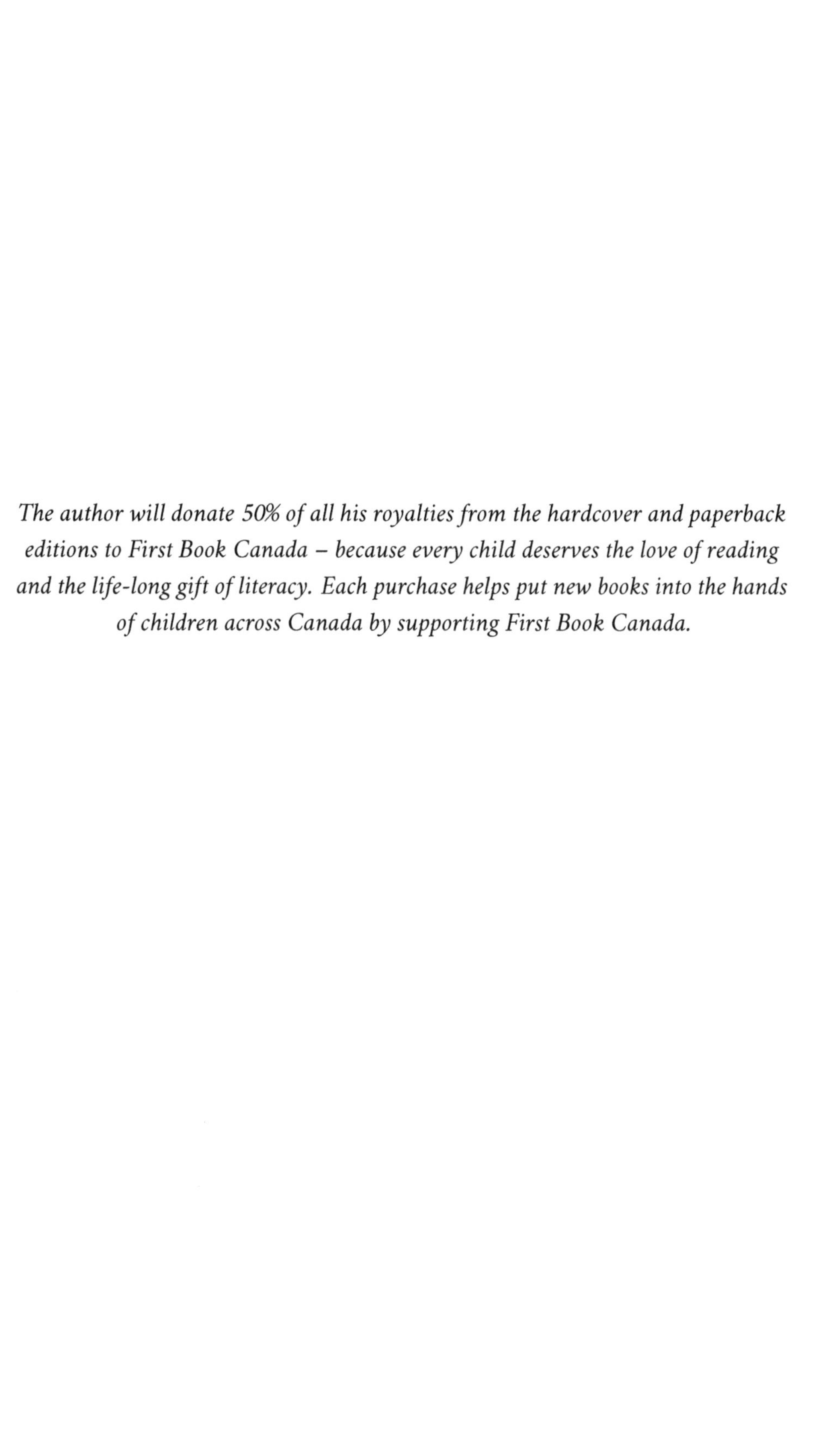

The author will donate 50% of all his royalties from the hardcover and paperback editions to First Book Canada – because every child deserves the love of reading and the life-long gift of literacy. Each purchase helps put new books into the hands of children across Canada by supporting First Book Canada.

Be kind whenever possible.
It is always possible.

Dalai Lama

Contents

Introduction – A Note to Parents and Caregivers

As a grandparent, I appreciate the importance of being able to help young children explore their imaginations, to learn while having fun, and to help those growing brains thrive.

These stories are written with young children in mind, though people of all ages may also find comfort as each story is wrapped with relaxing meditative guidance to help ease into a restful and restorative sleep.

The printed and eBook versions of this book will serve as the parent's script for bedtime storytelling, and you may choose to read the stories to young ones with or without the mindful relaxation guidance at the beginning and end of each story, though I encourage you to give the meditation guidance a try. You may discover that it works for you. The audiobook version of this book includes background music and sound effects which help set the mood and pacing in each story.

If these stories make you smile while entertaining the little ones at bedtime and if it makes you and them relax and sleep more soundly, then I will have achieved my goal. Perhaps it will also spark fruitful discussions with friends and family, or inspire a meditative practice beyond the chapters of this book.

This book is dedicated to young people everywhere, including my grandchildren, Sonali, Pariya, Deco and Elika. They unknowingly served as my candid focus group, always quick to identify anything in my stories that didn't sound right to them. My wife Micheline also provided sound advice, and I also appreciate her incredible patience as I spent countless hours pursuing this passion for storytelling. The beautiful royalty-free background music in the audiobook is generously provided via Pixabay, as are many of the images in the printed editions. A full list of credits for background music and images is included at the end of this book. I am tremendously grateful for the talented musicians and artists who have shared their creations.

Your purchase of the hardcover and paperback editions will support First Book Canada, helping put new books into the hands of children across Canada. I am also grateful to you for taking the time for self care, for sharing these stories with your loved ones.

Be well my friend,
Andy

The Angry Flower

Welcome to a bedtime story – *The Angry Flower*.

We'll get to this story in a minute… but first, let's get comfy.

Lay down in your bed, on your back, if that makes you feel comfortable right now.

Relax. Think about making your body soft like Jello.

If you need to, wiggle around a little bit so you're cozy.

Snuggle up to your soft blanket, or cuddly stuffed toy, if you have one.

Gently close your eyes.

You are safe here.

Now, notice your breathing. Slowly breathing in and out… Calmly….

Let's do three deep breaths together…. Slow deep breath in…. Slow, long, breath out….

Again Slow deep breath in…. Slow, long, breath out….

One last time. A slow deep breath in…. Long, breath out….

Well done… Now, just breathe naturally… continue noticing your breath….

With every breath out, you are more and more relaxed. More and more ready for sleep.

You may notice, your body, feeling heavier, … your head, feeling heavier, as it sinks, into the pillow….

Your back, softly sinking into the bed below you…. Your arms and legs, …also feeling heavier… and you are now feeling calm, cozy, relaxed, and sleepy.

Eyes closed.

You are safe here, as we begin our story, The Angry Flower.

It all happened to the young new flower one beautiful summer day. Young Lotus wasn't in a good mood this day. Young Lotus didn't know why, but something just didn't feel right. He was feeling a little impatient at times. He didn't tell his parent flower about the way he was feeling, either.

Things suddenly got worse, when a honey bee came buzzing near him.

Lotus didn't like the bee's buzzing sound. To Young Lotus, the bee seemed like a big monster, with mean eyes, and fast-moving wings. He thought it was coming to attack him. And when the bee landed on Lotus, it reached in to the center of the flower, and gathered some of the sweet, liquid nectar. The surprise made Lotus very angry. He felt the bee was stealing – and buzzing irritably as it collected the nectar from Lotus. The soft white and pink petals that usually made Lotus beautiful now darkened, into a deeper red as Lotus focused on his anger.

Lotus tried to rapidly flip its petals around, to swat the bee. But it got away swiftly, safely, and unhurt. Parent Lotus was watching as this happened, as the bee came by to gather some sweet nectar, and how young Lotus was suddenly upset, very red, very angry.

(Parent Lotus) "Now now, Lotus. Why are you angry?"

(Young Lotus) "Because the bee stole my nectar. I don't want that to happen. The nectar is mine! I'm never going to let a bee get close to me – never again!"

Young Lotus was furious. Parent Lotus knew about anger. And a parent knows, understanding anger, will help. Parent Lotus reached out to Young Lotus, and gave a nice squeezy hug. That made Young Lotus feel better already.

Parent Lotus asked, "Young Lotus, Tell me how it makes you feel inside, when you're angry."

Young Lotus thought about this wise question for a moment. He had not considered what was happening inside his body as the anger boiled up a few moments ago. He paused a minute to think about his experience. Young Lotus slowly gathered his thoughts and memories that led him to suddenly be angry, and after thinking about this – and as he spoke, he began to feel calmer, too.

(Young Lotus) "I think my heart just started beating really fast, and my breathing was shorter and choppy too. My flower head even felt hot! I think my anger just took over all of my other feelings. I wanted to stomp my feet or something. To jump right out of my roots and, maybe, even, hurt the bee. I was really upset because the bee was stealing from me. That nectar is mine…"

Parent Lotus was thankful that young Lotus took the time to think about his feelings. That is the first big step to learning how to control anger. It's the first step toward better understanding.

(Parent Lotus) "You did well to explain how you feel. It is OK to feel anger. Everyone does sometimes, even adults. – But it would not be OK to allow anger to take control – and in anger hurt someone."

(Young Lotus) "I know. But I felt like I had to protect myself… The bee was taking something from me…"

Parent Lotus felt now was the time to help young Lotus understand what was really happening at the time. "Young Lotus, did you know that we would not exist without bees?"

(Young Lotus) "What? No! Really?"

(Parent Lotus) "Bees visit flowers to gather nectar. That sweet liquid is what they bring back to the bees' nest to make honey. The honey is used to feed all the bees, including the baby bees. And, humans like to collect honey too. Humans like bees for that – but they also like bees because they are so important to all plants, including the Lotus family."

(Young Lotus) "Really? I didn't know they make honey. But Lotus flowers don't need honey. So, how can bees be good for us too?"

(Parent Lotus) "Well, when bees come by to gather nectar from flowers, they also are touching our petals, and other parts in the middle of our flowers. Did you notice any yellow powder on the legs of that bee?"

(Young Lotus) "Yes, I did. Their beating wings seemed to stir up the yellow powder, and some if it stayed on the bee's legs."

(Parent Lotus) "That dust on the bees legs is like magic – It is called pollen - the secret of life for all plants. When they go from flower to flower, some of the pollen dust also drops off on the flower - and that helps the flower make seeds – seeds that will eventually grow into more little flowers - just like you!"

(Young Lotus) "Wow. You mean, I wouldn't even be here today without the help of a bee?"

(Parent Lotus) "Exactly. Without bees – we would never have seeds that grow! Bees are so important to almost all plant life in the world! Bees are always busy working hard to keep the world full of beautiful plants – and of course, yummy honey for humans!"

Young Lotus was amazed at this new knowledge. He just learned more about bees – and now this instantly changed the way he thought of bees. Understanding more about something will do that. Now, he no longer would think of the bee as annoying, or even think of the bee's actions as stealing, as he thought earlier. Now, Young Lotus realized the bee was a friend – coming to get nectar as a reward for sharing pollen. The bee was doing important work for everyone!

Young Lotus thought about the first time he saw the bee, when he thought the eyes looked fierce and threatening – and he felt fear, and then anger. Now, he understands the bees eyes are just big - so they can see where the nectar is in a flower. And, their buzzing wings help them fly exactly where they need to be – to do an important job for all of nature.

(Young Lotus) "Bees are actually my friends. And they're so beautiful, with those black and yellow stripes and cute little legs full of pollen. I can't wait to share my nectar, next time!"

And just then, as Young Lotus was feeling so much better than when he felt angry earlier – another bee came by. Lotus was not angry this time. He let his beautiful white and pink petals shine brightly – to welcome the bee.

The bee smiled back, and wiggled sideways, left and right, a couple of times, as if to say hello, and thank you, to Young Lotus. How a little more understanding made all the difference!

Young Lotus thought, "Next time I feel anger coming up inside me, I'm just going to stop for a moment, take a deep breath, and take a few seconds to truly understand what is happening. It is probably not something threatening, and I just a need to understand more. I am so grateful that I had this talk with Parent Lotus."

Young Lotus was feeling great about his day. He had learned so much! And, that afternoon, three more bees actually came by to happily do their busy work for nature. Now, the sun was setting, so he knew it was time to close up the petals for the night, as flowers do when they get ready for sleep.

(Young Lotus) "Maybe there will be even more bees tomorrow!"

Young Lotus yawned… Ready for a peaceful and restful sleep.

Like Young Lotus, we all have had a great day, and so it is time to sleep… to recharge our bodies for another terrific day, just like this one, tomorrow.

So, let's slip into sleepytime now.

Eyes are closed…

and you are breathing….
slowly…
and calmly.
As you rest, sinking softly into your bed and pillow, continue thinking about your breathing…
No need to do anything… No need to think about anything else…
You are comfortable, Cozy, Ready, ….letting go of the day.
Slipping soundly into a deep, peaceful, and very restful, sleep.
It is time now… for pleasant, and sweet dreams.

Thank Your Lucky Stars

Welcome to a bedtime story - *Thank Your Lucky Stars*.

Get comfy now, as we get ready for this cosmic story. Cozy up now, into those soft, cuddly blankets, and a snuggly toy, if you have one.

Take in a long deep breath… then, let it out….

Good. Now just breath normally and relax.

Now it is time for our story about lucky stars.

"Star light, star bright, First star I see tonight, I wish I may, I wish I might, Have this wish I wish tonight."

You may have heard this short poem, that you say when you see the first star in the early evening. But have you ever heard the story about the stars that you do not see at night? They are the lucky stars. And here is their story.

You would be especially lucky, to find a lucky star. Because they are hiding in the most unlikely of places. Every thousand years or so, stars way up in the sky, will need a rest. They get tired after a thousand years of lighting up the evening sky. They shine brightly, hoping they will be your first "star light, star bright" to wish upon each night. When a star needs a rest, it will fall to earth. You may have heard about these falling stars before. When looking at the night sky, you may suddenly see a streak of bright light blazing across the sky. It all lasts only a second or so.

Some people will make a wish upon a falling star. Have you ever seen a falling star? Did you make a wish? It is the last wish that star will give, in the moment it begins falling to earth for a well-deserved rest. Once it has rested it will safely return to the night sky.

There is a falling star secret… only some ancient people had… many thousands of years ago. You will learn about the secret. Here. Tonight.

Our ancient ancestors knew that the sight of a falling star, was far more than a chance to make a wish, even though that is true. They learned that seeing a fallen star, is a secret signal that this moment is an ideal time to be quiet, calm, and to relax your mind. Why? Because it is the best time to listen to your thoughts… those tiny thought clouds that pop into your mind, then continue… until another thought arises. Even as you are quiet, calm, relaxed. In the moments after you see a falling star, your mind is ready, and in the peace and quiet – you may discover new ideas, new dreams, new wisdom.

The ancient ancestors have gained much wisdom over hundreds of years. In that time, they learned the most amazing secrets of the stars, including where the stars go – after they fall to Earth. And, they learned the stars fall to earth for a well-deserved, rest. Of all the billions of people who live on our planet Earth – and billions more who lived a long time ago – only a very small number have ever seen where the star goes to rest. I've heard this great secret, and now, I'm going to share it with you.

The tired star will find an old log in the forest. Like good friends, the tired star, and old tired tree log, will help each other. The log will release its energy as it slowly returns to the earth, and as it feeds other plants nearby with this energy, the resting star also recovers its own energy.

Finding a resting star in an old log is not easy. But here are some tips on finding a fallen star. You will need to walk into the forest, with an adult. Stars do like to hide in old logs near well-worn paths in the forest – so you won't need to leave the path at anytime. But you will need to be very alert, ready to spot something tiny and amazing.

If you see a fallen tree log laying down next to the path, you will have found one of the most favourite places for fallen stars to hide, while they rest. Not all logs will have fallen stars though. The star will only be found in a hollow log – one with a deep hole in the centre of the log, that will look like a tunnel. It is within this shadow of the hollow log that you might see a well-hidden star at rest. You may not notice the star, at first. Just like you, stars like to be snuggled in a cozy blanket while they sleep – and they wrap a leaf around them, as their blanket.

So, if you are very lucky, you might find a resting fallen star, wrapped in a red and orange maple leaf during the fall season, or another kind of leaf, at any other time of the year. The lucky star will be sleeping. So, if you do find a fallen star in a hollow log – be sure to stay quiet, so it continues, to rest, deeply.

The ancient ancestors learned a special secret about sleeping lucky stars. Their rest will be so much better if people can be calm, peaceful and in their minds, be thankful for the stars resting in our forests, and to include thanks and being grateful for other things too, while thinking about the star.

Can you think of things to be grateful for today? Did you have fun with friends or family? Did you have some delicious food? Was the weather comfortable today?

Of course, we must also be grateful for the sleeping lucky stars, for this gratitude to work as you think about those things in your mind. The ancient ancestors learned that being grateful for things made those things more likely to happen again. And, with the resting stars on Earth – if you thank your lucky stars – you will be helping it gain more energy – getting more rest.

Your gratitude will make each lucky star shine more brightly! Once it has fully rested, it will magically return to the skies. On the next beautiful sunny day, it will follow the sun's rays, all the way up into the sky. Once again, the lucky star will shine brightly in the night sky. You can do this, by being grateful, even if you never find one hiding, wrapped in a leaf, in a hollow log.

Know that your gratitude is helpful – to the lucky stars – to everyone around you, and even to yourself!

By thanking your lucky stars, you too, will shine more brightly, with happiness! Now that our gratitude has returned some lucky stars to the sky, we can also rest, and recharge.

Let's get comfy, so we can be ready for a good, restful, sleep.

Lay down in your bed, on your back, if that makes you comfortable. Think about making your body calm, relaxed.

Gently close your eyes.

You are safe here.

Now, notice your breathing. Thinking about your breathing, helps you relax.

Let's take three long deep breaths.

A deep breath in…. And, then a slow, long, breath out….

Again… deep breath in…. And, then a slow, long, breath out….

Very good!

One more time.

Deep breath in…. And, then a slow, long, breath out….

Eyes closed.

Calmly breathing.

You are ready, for a deep, restful sleep.

You are grateful, thankful, happy, for all the wonderful things, including the lucky stars.

Your body is feeling heavier… heavier… gently supported by the bed under you.

You feel relaxed.

You are comfy. Cozy. Safe.

It is time now… for pleasant, and sweet dreams.

Legend of the Fireflies

Welcome to a bedtime story - *Legend of the Fireflies.*
Not everyone has been fortunate enough to see the early evening sparks of a firefly – and even fewer people know the secrets behind the legend of the fireflies. I will share these secrets with you, here, tonight.

But first, let's get ready for bedtime.

As you lay down in your bed, begin to relax.

Imagine your body softening, from your head to your little toes.

And notice how you're feeling heavier as your head sinks comfortably into the pillow.

Your body, legs, and arms, settling softly into the cozy bed under you.

Now, gently close your eyes.

Nothing else to do now except relax, listening to my voice, as I begin the story.

Fireflies usually come out around bedtime, so many people, especially young people, have never seen one. You'll find fireflies hovering near the edge of forests and marshlands, and in some backyards, soon after the sun has gone down for the night. It has been said that you don't find fireflies – they find you! They only spark – with their tiny flashes of light – during the early part of summer.

And so, it was early one warm summer evening when Sonali and Pariya were finishing a game of hopscotch in the backyard, and they were about to go indoors when Pariya noticed a very short but bright spark near the shrubs at the back of the yard. What could it be?

Pariya told Sonali what she saw, so they thought about the possibilities. Could it be a falling star? They've heard stories about falling stars. And, wishing upon a falling star. But don't they come down directly from the stars above? Pariya saw the flash of light go sideways – as if it was going from one side of the yard – to the other. So it couldn't be that.

Sonali thought it could be a spark from a fireplace or distant forest fire. But they didn't smell or see smoke. So it wouldn't be that.

Then, suddenly, another spark appeared. Then another, and another! An amazing show of tiny lights, moving in one direction – then another — then vanishing. All in a second or two. Then, again… and again.

Pariya and Sonali watched the mysterious flying sparks, wondering what they could be, when from the yard next door – Fox called out to them, "So, I see you are watching the fireflies tonight!"

Fox knew about fireflies. But it was a new experience for Sonali and Pariya. First, Fox pointed out that fireflies aren't flies at all. In fact, they're a special kind of beetle. He also explained that fireflies have a magical power – called bio luminescence – that can make their bodies blink with light. They only do this in the early evening – and only during a few weeks of the year. But the most magical thing about the fireflies, Fox told them, is what their sparks of light have taught people around the world – for thousands of years.

Fox told Pariya and Sonali that ancient people who lived a long time ago, passed on the legend of the fireflies, as it exists to this day. They learned that the mysterious blinking light of fireflies – are a source of healing energy and may have a special superpower to make wishes come true – especially wishes that help others.

Sonali realized the blink of a firefly is a lot like the flash of light from a falling star – and people have been wishing on falling stars for hundreds of years.

And, Pariya remembers her grandfather mentioning how plants in the garden grow because of the light that comes from the sun – even though the sun is far, far, away. She wondered, could the light of fireflies be helping people grow too?

Fox said he was certain all these kinds of light – from the sun, falling stars, and fireflies, were positive energy that is everywhere in the universe. And they wondered, if it is everywhere - could people also have – and share - this good energy?

Just as they were thinking about this – a bunch of fireflies sparked up all around them, almost making the yard around them glow in the warmth of their beautiful loving light. It was as if the fireflies were sending them a message. Maybe people can also share this energy of the universe!

Fox said the ancient people learned from the fireflies that we can use our minds to imagine sending healing energy, love and compassion to others, and that we could do so during meditation. He said it is still a common meditation practice today.

Soon, the flurry of firefly sparks went away. Maybe it was their bedtime, too. Sonali and Pariya thanked Fox for sharing his knowledge of the legend of the fireflies. They had learned a lot tonight. It was nearing bedtime, so as the three said their goodbyes and began to go back inside their homes for a good restful sleep, they all agreed they would try tonight, to imagine sending light filled with love and compassion to the people they love. Even if they don't glow like a firefly.

At the end of this day, as they snuggled into their beds, they were now ready for a restful sleep.

As they slowly calmed their minds – they imagined sending a person they love some of the same magical light that the fireflies shared with them.

You may even want to think about sending your healing light and love to someone special to you.

Just like Sonali, Pariya and Fox.
Just like the ancient people.
Just like the fireflies.

You can also slip into sleepytime, anytime now.

Gently close your eyes.

Now, let's take a big deep breath to help us settle into sleepytime. Take a deep breath in - filling your whole body with all that good energy. Then let all that air out – long breath out.

Let all thoughts of the day, float far, far, away.

If you wish, keep watching your breath in and out… and with every breath, feeling more and more relaxed.

You are now ready for a deep and restful sleep.

It is time now, for pleasant and sweet dreams.

Secret Superpowers in my Sleep

This is a story, about your secret, sleepytime, superpowers.

You may not even know it. You have superpowers while you sleep!

Have you ever tried to fall asleep, but could not, no matter how hard you tried? Maybe you felt too excited, about the day. Or, maybe, you just felt like moving around. That's OK. Everyone has difficulty getting to sleep, sometimes.

This story will help you learn ways to get set for sleep, and learn about the superpowers you have while you are asleep.

Now, before I talk about your sleepy time superpowers and getting ready for sleep, let's get comfy.

Lay down in your bed, on your back, if that makes you feel comfortable right now.

Relax.
Think about making your body comfortable. If you need to, wiggle around a little bit so you're relaxed, and cozy.
Snuggle up to your soft blanket, or cuddly stuffed toy, if you have one.
Gently close your eyes.
You are safe here.

Now, notice your breathing. Slowly breathing in and out, calmly.
Slow deep breaths in... Long, slow, breaths out...
Softly place your hand on your tummy. Breathing. Notice how your tummy goes up slightly when you breathe in, and down gently when you breathe

out.
Thinking about your breathing helps you to relax. It helps tell your body and brain, to get ready for sleep.
As you breathe, you may notice, your body, feeling heavier. Your head, feeling heavier, as it sinks, into the pillow.

Your back, feeling heavier as it sinks into the bed under you. Your arms and legs, also feeling heavier, and you are now feeling calm, and relaxed. Continue noticing your breathing.

Good. As you do this, you are gently activating your sleepytime superpowers, as you relax, more and more, with each and every breath.

You are safe here.

Eyes closed, as you get ready for your sleepytime super powers.

Your first sleepytime superpower actually could begin before you are laying down. What you do before bedtime, makes a difference in how ready you are for sleep.

Your first superpower is called sleep hygiene. Hygiene is a big word for being healthy and clean; in the same way that you may wash your hands and brush your teeth, before bedtime. You can have sleepy time hygiene - a secret superpower - in the time before bed.

Staying away from screen time, away from watching computers, phones and television, increase your superpowers, for sleep. Those screens are bright lights, and they send a signal to your brain to stay awake. So, you do not want these signals, right before bedtime.

You also do not want to eat too much, before bedtime – especially a huge meal, and desserts or other sweet treats – as our superpowers are not as powerful, on a full tummy.

Going to bed at the same time each night, also helps your sleepytime superpowers. They'll be ready at the same time each night. We don't want to keep our superpowers waiting, too long, by staying up too late!

As you prepare for bedtime, you can activate your secret sleepytime superpowers – using your imagination… to think about your breathing… to think about being calm… and relaxing… slowing down… before sleep. These superpowers shift your body and mind into a lower gear… relaxing your body… calming your mind… on your way to a deep, and restful, sleep.

Most of what happens, when we are sound asleep, we will not actually remember. We might be lucky enough to remember some of our dreams. Especially the fun dreams.

Some people are able to make their dreams even more fun, by thinking nice things before, and during, sleep.

Try it.

Dreams are not real – but they may seem real while you are sleep. With practice, you will know this, while you are sleeping. It's a superpower that takes practice, and in time you too, might make all your dreams, really fun!

Next time you're near the ocean in your dream, see if you can swim with the dolphins. Next time you are exploring space in your dream, become an astronaut on a space walk. And when you dream about animals, imagine any playful pet you want. With your dream superpowers, you can ride dinosaurs, and fly with the eagles, and have a long talk with your pet dog, cat or rabbit! You can do anything while you sleep.

Making up dreams, is only one way your body is busy at work while you sleep. You have so many more superpowers.

While you sleep, your brain is actively thinking all about the day you just had. It's almost like your brain is playing a movie about the day, all over again, and it will keep those memories for later, whenever you want to think about the fun you had today.

As you sleep, if there was something you couldn't figure out today – your brain may even come up with an answer, that will suddenly, pop into your mind, sometime the next day.

Your brain does not rest during sleep. It is busy while you sleep. Its superpowers are solving puzzles while you rest, coming up with answers to your daytime questions, and solutions to any daytime problems.

Your brain's superpowers do this, even while you are sound asleep! The rest of your body is also putting into action its secret superpowers, turning the good foods you've been eating today, into larger bones and teeth, as you grow, and into stronger muscles too. While you sleep, your superpowers are stopping any germs it may find, so you will not get sick, and fixing any bumps and bruises that may have happened, healing anywhere you need healing.

Have you ever noticed that sleep seems so short? As if you only close your eyes, and then, it is morning already? You may think about this now – if you're still wanting to stay awake, or wanting to continue, with some of the things, you were doing today. You may still do some of those things again, tomorrow! And tomorrow, comes quickly – it seems - almost as soon as you fall asleep.

The more quickly you fall asleep – the more quickly the next day will seem to arrive. So, allowing yourself a refreshing, deep, sleep - is the fast way, to get to all of those exciting things, you hope to do tomorrow.

Once you are laying in bed… body feeling heavier… and relaxing… cozy, and comfy… noticing your breathing… your sleepytime superpowers get to work as you rest.

Your sleepytime superpowers are getting you set for the next day, secretly supercharging your body for tomorrow, secretly preparing you, to be in a good mood, to be happy and thankful for another terrific day.

You are your own body's superhero!

You may slip into deep sleep easily, anytime now. And that is OK. Your sleepytime superpowers… are ready!

So, let's slip into sleepy time now.

Eyes are closed… and you are breathing… slowly… and calmly.

You are comfortable.

Cozy.

Ready.

Letting go of the day.

It is time now, for pleasant, and sweet, restful, dreams.

The Best Presents Ever

Welcome to a bedtime story: *The Best Presents Ever*.

I am so happy you are here for this ancient tale about one of the best presents ever given. This secret comes from wise people who lived thousands of years ago. Long before stores and online shopping existed, they knew about the most meaningful presence.

Before we get to this story, let us get comfy.

Cozy up now, into those soft, cuddly blankets, and a snuggly toy, if you have one. Feel yourself sinking into the bed under you, as you settle in for this tale from years long ago.

Take in a few long deep breaths as you settle in. With each breath in, imagine a wave of healthy energy coming into your body. And as you let each breath go, you are letting go of anything you no longer need.
Nothing to do. Nothing to worry about. Just listen to my voice.
Just breathe, normally. And relax. Very good.

Now, it is time for our story, about the best presents - ever.

Serena was worried. She had had an argument with one of her favourite friends at school. She did not intend to have an argument – but she had stopped listening to her friend Alden, as her mind drifted to thinking about other things. Have you ever stopped listening, this way? Maybe you were thinking of the next thing you were going to say?

Her friend Alden was always so calm. He seemed to think for a second or two, every time he had something to say. And, when he spoke, it always seemed important. It was obvious he had listened to every word Serena said, before he would talk.

Serena felt bad that she interrupted Alden earlier that day, as he was trying to explain a rule for a game they were playing. She did not understand at the time that he was just trying to be helpful. Alden seemed hurt that she was not listening, yet he was kind enough to say she would learn about the game's rules, on her own, one day.

Still, Serena was worried this argument would not be good for their friendship. She was worried they might stop being friends. At first, she thought about buying something to show she was sorry for the argument. She had seen how sometimes adults will buy something after having an argument, to try to make the other person feel better, for a few minutes.

It was not a traditional holiday, or even Alden's birthday, but she thought, maybe a gift for Alden would help her say sorry. What would be the best present she could get for Alden? Serena felt she just had to find and buy the best present ever. Where would she find it?

She used her Mom's laptop to try online shopping, but nothing she searched seemed like a good idea. Then, she went to the local shopping mall – and realized that nothing could make up for that argument. There was no present she could bring to school the next day, to give Alden, to say sorry.

As she lay in her bed at the end of a long shopping day – she felt frustrated. Worried. But then, she remembered something Alden once told her, when she was wondering how he always seemed so calm, and why he was able to never interrupt her when she spoke.

Alden mentioned that, in ancient times, the wise people then knew the best gift ever – and it was not any thing you could buy. They could never put these best presents ever, in a package, or even hold it in their hands. It did not require money – but it did require having patience, razor-sharp awareness, and self-control.

She now remembered the ancient secret. She remembered Alden had said, for thousands of years, the wise elders knew that the best present ever – was a thing called, presence.

Presence – was when one is being present in the moment, like here, now.

Serena was excited and encouraged as she remembered this ancient wisdom. She made a promise to herself: From now on, she would do her best to be fully aware, fully engaged in others, to listen to what they were saying instead of thinking about the next thing she would say – or interrupting. She would do her best to understand, by being mindful and focused in the present moment.

The next day, as she arrived at school, Serena was no longer worried. She confidently walked up to Alden, and said, "Sorry." for the argument. Then she said, "Thank you," too. She was grateful the argument made her remember the ancient secret called presence. She then repeated her promise to Alden, to always do her best to give him her presence – her full attention in the present moment. From now on, Serena promised, she would listen instead of thinking about the next thing she would say – or even blurting it out before he finished talking, as she did the day of the argument.

Not surprisingly, wise Alden listened calmly, and smiled happily, the entire time she spoke to him. Serena noticed how he was so skilled at never interrupting her.

When Alden finally spoke, she listened fully, now keeping her promise. He told Serena he valued her friendship and the earlier conversation she worried about didn't bother him as much as it did her.

She listened mindfully as she practiced being fully engaged, fully present, and realized that doing so meant enjoying their conversation much more fully. They were now able to play without misunderstandings. They would now pay attention to the other's emotions, and of their own emotions. And with this new understanding, they could even solve problems together more easily.

Their friendship connection was now stronger than ever. Now, as they played, mindfully present and fully aware in the moment, they continued to create lasting memories each day. For Serena, learning about presence was the best present ever.

Could it be yours, too? Could you try to have complete presence with others tomorrow? Let's engage in the present moment now, as we get ready for a deep restful sleep.

Nothing to do, or to think about now.

Let's get comfy.

Lying down in your bed.

Think about making your body calm, relaxed.

Gently close your eyes.

You are safe here.

Now, notice your breathing. Thinking about your breathing, helps you relax.

Fresh healthy energy in every breath in…. and letting out what you no longer need, with every breath out….

Let's take three long deep breaths. A deep breath in…. And, then a slow, long, breath out….

Again… deep breath in…. And, then a slow, long, breath out…. Very good!

One more time, deep breath in…. And, then a slow, long, breath out….

Eyes closed.

Calmly breathing.

You are ready to have complete presence with others, tomorrow.

It is the best present ever, being present in each moment.

And, now you are ready, for a deep, restful sleep.

Your body is feeling heavier… heavier… gently supported by the bed under you.

You feel relaxed.

You are comfy. Cozy. Safe.

It is time now… for pleasant, and sweet dreams.

Picnic Mountain and the Leaning Bench

Welcome to a bedtime story - *Picnic Mountain and the Leaning Bench.*

Have you ever gone on a long hike through the forest, and all the way to the top of a mountain?
We will use our imaginations to do just that, here, tonight.

Before we get to this story, let us get comfy, snuggling in to your cuddly blankets, hugging your stuffed toy if you have one.

Feel yourself sinking into the bed under you, as you settle in for this story, before a deep restful sleep.
Now just relax, noticing your breathing.
As you breath in, can you feel how your belly rises slightly? And as you breath out – exhale a longer breath, letting go of all the old air and anything from the day you no longer need.

There is nothing to do now.
Not thinking about the day, not worrying about tomorrow.
Just listening to my voice.

Now, it is time for the story about an amazing place called Picnic Mountain – and the secrets of the leaning bench that rests at the top of the mountain.

It was first discovered – a long, long, time ago… that being at the top of a mountain could be enlightening. Being at the summit might help solve great mysteries, bringing about new understanding. Elika had heard about this, so she and her cousin Deco decided one autumn day to explore Picnic Mountain. It was to be an adventure they would remember.

Before they headed out to Picnic Mountain, they first told their parents about their plans, and of course, they each packed a small picnic lunch with a sandwich, a bottle of water, and an apple. Deco and Elika had lots of practice walking on long hikes with their grandfather, so the ambitious walk from the base of the mountain to the top seemed easy enough to them.

They knew that enjoying the journey was just as important as the destination. They noticed the leaves of the trees at the base of the mountain were already beginning to change colour, as they do in the fall in this part of the world.

Maple trees display some of the most beautiful orange and reds ever seen on plants, though the reds of big oak trees, and the blazing yellow leaves of the beech tree also beautifully paint the forest path up Picnic Mountain.

Elika and Deco walked slowly, taking time to notice many of the different kinds of plants along the way. There were tall trees, and tiny shrubs. There were ferns, mosses and fungus. All different shapes and sizes. They also kept a lookout for poison ivy or stinging nettle – which can cause a very uncomfortable itch and rash.

They also noticed a few creatures along the way, like the robin on a birch tree branch. The usual bugs like beetles and those mosquitoes, and colourful fluttering butterflies.

A young cottontail bunny hopped along nearby, with mostly brown fur with tufts of white as it readies for the coming winter months. As the bunny vanished into the bush, a red squirrel called out – as if it was wanting them to notice him too.

Then, about half-way up the mountain, a raccoon sauntered slowly across their path. It was as surprised to see humans as Elika and Deco were surprised to see it. Staring at the two with its dark round eyes surrounded with its dark furry mask, the raccoon seemed harmless from a distance. Elika knew to stay still when seeing such animals, rather than scaring it away, or making it feel threatened.

Raccoons are also known as wash bears in some parts of the world, because of the way they appear to wash their food in water before eating. The raccoons, or wash bears, may not actually be washing their food. Their tiny paws sense the food more when their hands are wet, so by holding their food in water may be more alert to the texture and quality of the food they're eating. Deco thought about that for a moment and imagined that they will try to be more aware when they have a picnic at the top of Picnic Mountain.

Climbing the last stretch to the top of the mountain was more challenging, as the hillside was increasingly steep. Reaching a goal is often a challenge – yet worth the effort. Elika and Deco stayed determined along the steep path, pausing at times to rest, and to notice that the air was getting hazy, like a fog. Or perhaps they were getting closer to the clouds? Could they even be in a cloud?

Elika could see what appeared to be old wooden log steps, built into the mountainside – a clear sign that they were nearing the summit – or top of the mountain. And a few moments later, there it was. The Leaning Bench! They had hiked and climbed all the way to the top of Picnic Mountain.

They took in a deep breath of the fresh mountain air, which smelled like the nearby pine trees at the top of picnic mountain. They sat on the leaning bench. Sitting still, even though the bench leaned forward ever so slightly, but not enough for them to fall off. At first the two just sat there, in silence.

It was so foggy – surrounded by the mountain cloud – they could barely see anything downhill. But they could hear – the distant sound of a barred owl. Many say owls are wise, and hearing it at the summit of Picnic Mountain seemed like the perfect place for wisdom.

Deco remembered the raccoon – and his thoughts about mindful eating. It was time for their picnic.

As they started eating their sandwiches, Elika felt there was something magical about eating food in the open air. Every bite seemed better than the last, as they both chewed their food slowly. They savoured the rich flavours in every small bite. Elika and Deco were both being very mindful, and very aware.

They remembered how their grandfather talked about mindfulness, awareness and about meditation. So, as they finished their picnic. They sat, still, and silent, on the leaning bench. Listening to the sound of the wind rustling the leaves. They were completely relaxed. Sitting there. They softly closed their eyes, sensing the dense fog around them. For a few minutes, they had nothing else to do, nothing else to think about. Except the present moment. They were fully aware – not distracted about the past or thinking about the future. On the leaning bench, they were leaning into the present moment.

And then, the cool dampness of the fog they were feeling was being swept aside in the breeze and replaced with the welcoming warmth of sunshine. Deco and Elika opened their eyes and saw that the cloud at the summit of

Picnic Mountain was suddenly lifting. The beautiful clear blue sky was now everywhere around them. At Picnic Mountain – this was a feast for the eyes! They wondered, could this be what is meant by enlightenment?

Now, they could see the rest of the mountain area more clearly than ever before – appreciating with more awareness every plant and animal they saw as they made their way back down the mountain toward home. Did the stillness at leaning bench awaken some superpower in them?

Maybe it was only a change in the weather, or perhaps it was magic as they sat in stillness on the leaning bench and the skies cleared as their minds began to see more clearly.

They couldn't wait until bedtime, when Deco and Elika would tell their families about the transformation they felt atop Picnic Mountain that day.

Let's also engage in the present moment now, as we too, get ready for a deep restful sleep.

Let's get comfy. Cozy. Safe.
Gently close your eyes.
Nothing to do, or to think about now.
Your body is feeling calm. Ready to rest.
Notice your breathing. Every breath in bringing in fresh healthy energy. With

every breath out, letting out what you no longer need.

Like Elika and Deco, you will be ready to eat mindfully and have more awareness, tomorrow.

For now, you are ready, for a deep, restful sleep.

It is time now… for pleasant, and sweet dreams.

Exploring the Ocean

In the next few minutes, we'll close our eyes and imagine a trip into the ocean – where all kinds of fish and plant life are waiting for you to discover them!

Don't worry, you won't need to hold your breath, or even know how to swim – since we're going there in our minds – our imagination!

Before we explore the depths of the ocean, let's take time to get comfy.

Laying down in your bed, or where-ever you feel comfortable, right now.
Snuggle up to your soft blanket or cuddly stuffed toy if you have one.
Now, just think about your body.
Let's get cozy and comfortable.
Ready to deeply relax.
Just wiggle around until you feel just right.

Notice how it feels to lay down, your head feeling heavier on the pillow, your back sinking heavily into the bed, and your arms and legs weighing down your body, into the bed under you.

You are safe here.

As you breathe now, relaxing, just notice as your belly rises softly with each breath in… and drops softly with each breath out….
Let's take a few deep breaths in… And slightly longer slow breaths out….
Again. Breathe in… breathe out….
One more time. Breathe in… breathe out….
Notice your breathing….

And, gently close your eyes.

Now is the time for your imagination to see and hear our swim into the deep ocean.

Tonight, you will have special superpowers, and you can swim quickly, and you can even breath underwater. You are comfortable, and safe.

We begin with a walk along the white sandy beach on a warm, sunny, summer day. The sand feels soft under your feet and between your toes as you walk closer to the waves.

You see a large leather back sea turtle also wobbling its way to the salty water, about to depart on its own ocean journey. Its flippers push sand aside, as its heavy shell body slides ever closer to the ocean.

Seabirds are flying overhead, squawking things only birds understand. They're swooping up and down in the gentle breeze, as the waves brush the shore. At times, the birds dive from high above and straight down into the water – trying to catch tiny fish for lunch.

Along the shore, where the waves are frothing white and gently sweeping the sand, you see a little orange crab, crawling side-ways, and a tiny starfish is moving its five outstretched arms, just under the shallow water at the edge of the ocean.

With your special superpowers during this story time, you are able to walk into the ocean, and begin swimming below the waves. The superpowers in this story allow you to breathe underwater, just for this story time.

In the distance, you see that large sea turtle, again. The turtle looks back at you, remembers you, and waves its flipper for you to join, and so you follow, swimming out into the ocean, deeper, and deeper.

Soon, you and the sea turtle are joined by three dolphins, and you swim deeper, still. The dolphins are playful, swimming up and down – almost playing a game of tag with each other — and they spin quickly as they soar toward the surface of the ocean, shooting above the waves for a moment before diving back into the water.

As the dolphins swim further away, you notice colourful patterns in the distance, and you swim toward it. As you approach, you recognize it to be a coral reef. You're amazed that the rainbow of colours – red, green, blue and more, slowly comes into focus — as shapes you know.

A variety of little fish swimming together like a cloud in motion.

An orange-tinted octopus. You can count all eight arms.

And then, a pink and purple jellyfish slowly hops by, seemingly bouncing up and down as it follows the ocean current.

And you even see a grayish, friendly-looking, shark.

They're all swimming around in a colourful mix of sea grasses and coral. So much life is here. Though coral reefs make up just a small part of the ocean, they are home to a large number of all living fish and plants in the ocean.

You stop swimming over the coral for a few minutes to watch all the life here. The coral reef and sponge corals are also home to tiny creatures sometimes peeking out of their miniature shells. The little creatures stick their heads out of their tiny shells, then hide. Stick their heads out, then hide, again. You imagine they're playing an ocean game of hide and seek.

Now, the sea turtle catches your attention once more, as it waves its flippers, inviting you to come along. And you do.

You continue to discover amazing sights during your swim.

A giant squid sails by overhead as you follow your turtle friend, its long fins stretching below its body as it sweeps its way through the ocean.

You also pass by an area where the rocks along the ocean's bottom reveal a cave. And in it, you see a magical light show – very tiny creatures that shine in the dark, creating their own light – or to use a very big word: bio luminescence!

Up above, a school of mackerel looks like a silvery cloud – blocking the sunshine for only a few seconds, and then you see the largest ocean creature of all.

In fact, the largest creature in the whole world! It is a blue whale, and it slowly arches its gigantic body, as it gracefully travels through the ocean. This huge gentle animal is longer than a jet plane and is heavier than two school buses! The whale rises up to the surface, and a large blast of water jets out from the spout on the top of its head. The whale continues to sail away, calling out to other blue whales that may be far, far away.

You can see the sun above the ocean waves has now lowered to the west, and the sky is becoming a fuzzy, pale, orange. As the sun sets, you think it best to return home now. All this ocean exploration has made you tired.

So, your giant turtle friend helps, as you hold onto its shell, and it pulls you through the ocean as you wave bye to the coral reef, the whale and other fish in the sea. On the sandy shore, you yawn. You're very tired now. And you know that sleep tonight will be filled with fond memories of this awesome tour of the seas.

Arriving home, you get ready for bed, and for a restful, deep, sleep, remembering your time exploring the ocean, and knowing there will be more fun days, just like this one.

Relax where you lay now.
You are safe.
Comfortable in your bed.
And with each breath in… and each breath out… you let go of the day…
Ready now for pleasant, sweet, dreams.

Exploring the Universe

In the next few minutes, we'll close our eyes together and imagine a trip, away from planet Earth, through the universe – with the moon, planets, stars and more, awaiting your discovery!

Relax.

You won't need to pack a lunch or go to the store to buy a spacesuit – because you're going there… in your mind. Pretending. Using your imagination!
Now, before we explore the vast universe, let's take time, to get comfy.

Lay down in your bed, or where-ever you feel comfortable right now.
Snuggle up to your soft blanket, or cuddly stuffed toy, if you have one.
Let's get cozy and comfortable.
Ready to deeply relax.
And just wiggle around if you need to, until you feel just right.
Notice how it feels to lay down, relaxing.
Your head feeling heavier on the pillow, your back sinking heavily into the bed, and your arms and legs weighing down your body, sinking softly into the bed under you.
As a young astronaut, you can pretend gravity is weighing you down.

You are safe here.

Now let's notice our breathing.
As you breathe now, relaxing, notice as your belly rises softly with each breath in… and drops softly with each breath out….
We'll take a few deep breaths in… And slightly, longer, slow, breaths, out….
Breathe in… breathe out….
Again. Breathe in… breathe out….
Good, now continue to notice your breathing, and gently close your eyes.

Now is the time for your imagination to see and hear our rocket ship launch into space toward the stars!

You are all dressed in a super safe and shiny astronaut suit, and, sitting safely buckled up in the pilot's chair. You're ready to launch your rocket. And push the red button to start the rocket engines.

As the countdown begins, you feel comfortable, and safe.

9… 8… 7… You're wondering what exploring space will be like, and what leaving planet Earth will be like.

6… 5… 4 … The rumbling of your rocket engines firing up begin to gently shake you. All this is normal for an astronaut, and you're safe.

3… 2…1… And blastoff! Your powerful rocket is now soaring, climbing through the skies, the atmosphere, and beyond!

Through the spaceship's window, you can see your home, all the buildings in the city, and country, getting farther and farther away. You see the oceans too, getting smaller as you go higher above our beautiful blue and green planet Earth. To boldly explore the solar system!

You've NEVER been this far from home! But you know you'll be back soon.

Now, you're also feeling lighter, as gravity slips away, and your seat belt keeps you from floating around.

You see how our planet is round, as it gets smaller and smaller… as you travel deeper… and deeper… into space. Soon, you're flying past satellites – and then you see the International Space Station. You wave to one of the astronauts looking out of her window as your rocket goes by.

A few seconds later, you're zooming by the moon, and you see the bumps and craters on the moon's surface, with a clarity that wasn't possible from home on planet Earth. The moon is not as nice as Earth, with its thick forests, sandy beaches and lush gardens. Our home planet feels very special.

The view from space is quite different, and with cosmic wonder, you view a night sky, like never before. In the distance, you see a comet. It is a bright, racing, chunk of ice with a long blue-green tail of frozen steam and dust. You see the comet now, how lucky! But by tomorrow, it may be in another solar system – another part of the universe, far, far, away.

And the stars even seem brighter from your spaceship. There are no clouds or atmosphere in the way to dim the view. Some of the stars you see are a bright white. Others blue. Others pink. Others greenish. Each tiny, shiny, spec in the universe looks only like a dot to our eyes. But each star, is as large as the Sun, and each star, may have its own, solar system, with its own planets and moons!

There are way too many stars to count. Millions. Maybe billions. Or gazillions! You can also see a long cluster of stars, known as 'the milky way'. The millions of stars look a bit like milk being poured across the universe, and it is so vast, that it would take thousands of light years just to travel to the center of the milky way. So, we're not going there tonight.

You also notice a giant circle of huge rocks going all the way around the sun – just like all the planets, including Earth. Some of the big rocks are small enough to hold in your hand. Others are as big as a house. They're called asteroids, and the asteroid belt floats through space like an enormous rocky merry-go-round!

Your exploration continues, as your rocket soars past some of our own solar system's planets. Outside the window to your left, toward the sun, you see, Mercury and Venus, and they seem grayish in colour, and you see Mars, and it is red. Looking out the window to your right, Jupiter appears brown and orange. Saturn is a pale gold with rings of red and white. No other planet seems to have these colourful rings, and you notice that Saturn also has many colourful moons.

You wonder, "What would it be like to live on these planets?", and after thinking about this a while, it makes you feel more like returning to our own, beautiful, blue and green, planet Earth. It's the special place in our solar system, we call home.

You gently turn the rocket back toward home. As the rocket lands, back on planet Earth, you realize all this space exploration, has been exhausting. So, you remove the astronaut suit, and you're happy to be home.

You yawn, tired now after a busy day, that was truly out of this world! And, you know that sleep, tonight, will be filled with fond memories, of this awesome tour of the solar system.

You are now ready for bed, and for a restful, deep, sleep.

Dreams will be fresh with memories of your time exploring, and knowing there will be more fun days, just like this one.

Relax where you lay now.

You are safe.

Cozy and Comfortable.

At home. On planet Earth.

And with each breath in… and each breath out… you let go of the day.

And you are ready now for pleasant, sweet, dreams.

Exploring the Forest

In the next few minutes, we'll close our eyes and imagine a walk in the forest – where interesting animals and plants are waiting for you to discover them! Now, before we go for our sunny day walk into the woods, let's take time to get comfy.

Lay down in your bed, or where-ever you feel comfortable right now.

Snuggle up in your soft blanket or cuddly stuffed toy, if you have one.

Notice how it feels to lay down. Just think about your body, getting ready, to deeply relax. If you need to, wiggle your body around, until you feel just right. Your head is feeling heavier on the pillow, your back sinking heavily into the bed, and your arms and legs weighing down your body, into the bed under you.

You are safe here.

As you breathe, relaxing, notice as your belly, rises softly, with each breath in… and drops softly with each breath out….
Take a few deep breaths in …. And slightly longer slow breaths out….
Again. Breathe in… breathe out.
Very good. Now, one more time.
Breathe in… Breathe out….
As you breathe now, just notice your breathing.
It will help you to relax.
And be sure to close your eyes.

Now is the time for your imagination to see, and hear, and even smell our stroll into the forest.

If you have a favourite playground with a forest nearby, you can think about that place now. Or, you can pretend, with your imagination… and I will help you discover.

On this beautiful sunny day, you see a path, at the edge of the forest, where you see short, leafy, trees like alder bushes, and birch trees. It is a happy and safe place to go – and the leafy shrubs are the first things you see, but there's so much more to explore!

As you walk along the path, you notice the trees get taller. The leaves of large maple trees sway in the warm gentle breeze, and the giant, needly pine trees reach up toward the sky. The sun's rays peek through the tree tops, all the way down to the ground, lighting your way along the forest path.

It smells like a forest, fresh & healthy air as you breathe in.

The pine trees have long dark-green needles on their branches, instead of leaves like the other trees you saw earlier. And, instead of flowers, they have pine cones. In those little brown pine cones, tiny seeds are getting ready to fall to earth, or perhaps the seeds will be carried on a windy day, to create new pine trees far away.

Now, you hear a "knock, knock, knock" over there, and you see a small woodpecker, pecking the bark on the side of one of the largest pine trees. The woodpecker is coloured black, with some white marks on its back feathers, and is mostly white on its belly. Its' head also has one bright red spot, on the top. With its short black beak, it is quickly picking tiny bugs off the tree. Pecking, "knock, knock, knock." And you wonder, "How can he do that without getting a headache?", as he pecks away so swiftly.

Then, the woodpecker stops, suddenly, and looks over toward you. You smile, as it examines you. Maybe it is the first time seeing a human! After a few seconds, it feels safe, and goes back to pecking, "knock, knock, knock."

Then, as you continue walking along the path, you hear something that brings your attention to a lower-lying area of the forest. You see short ferns, fanning out their green finger-like leaves. But something is moving those leaves! The ferns jiggle. Stop. Then jiggle again. Stop. Something is moving under there, making the fern leaves shake slightly at times. What could it be?

Soon you see!

It is a bunny, hopping under the ferns. Its fur has now turned from its winter coat of white, to a brownish colour that almost matches the colour of the ground. Bunnies sometimes change colour so they can be safely camouflaged, so they can hide. But this bunny doesn't seem concerned about you being there, and you calmly watch the bunny hop around for a little while, as it looks for food; foods like clover and other delicious leafy plants – and for yummy berries, like wild raspberries.

You hear the slight trickle of a brook just down the path where there is a small clearing… and imagine the sunny spot might be a good place for the bunny – and you – to find some red, tasty raspberries. The bunny follows you, along the path, to the sunny clearing, and you find some raspberries growing there, thickly hanging with ripe clusters of red and juicy berries.

You pick a few that are too high for the bunny to reach, and gently lower your freshly picked handful of berries, and you offer the bunny a snack. It waits still, for a moment, then cautiously, moves closer to your outstretched handful, and finally, nibbles a few of those yummy berries.

Do you feel happy being this close to nature?

As you think about this friendly and joyful moment with the bunny, you collect another handful of raspberries. These berries, you will take home, to wash and eat, later.

And you're feeling tired now. So, you take in another big breath of the clean forest air – and breathe in the fresh scent of the tall pine trees. And you begin to walk back along the path toward home.

There is always more to notice in the forest, even on the way back. You see a small green frog on the path ahead of you, but, as soon as he notices you, he jumps into the tall weeds to hide. Now you notice, a small dragonfly, blue and shiny, hovering over a bright yellow flower; with its tiny four wings buzzing like a mini helicopter. Then, the dragonfly lands on the flower. Perhaps to take a rest, or to smell the flower.

Do you feel lucky, and happy, to see the dragonfly this closely?

As you continue along the path, you notice the sun is getting lower now, and bedtime, is soon.

Arriving home, you get ready for bed, and for sleep, remembering your fantastic time, and discoveries while exploring the forest. The pine trees. The bunny. Raspberries and dragonflies. What a day!

You now have so many happy memories of this exploring day in the forest.

And you are ready to go to sleep now, knowing, there will be more fun days, just like this one.

Relax, where you lay now.
Your eyes are closed.
You are safe.
And you are comfortable.
And with each breath in… and each breath out…
You let go of the day.
Ready now for pleasant, sweet, dreams.

School Days Ahead

Welcome to a bedtime story – *School Days Ahead*!

We'll get to this story in a minute… but first, let's get cozy.

As you lay down in your bed, begin to relax.

Imagine your whole body softening.

Letting your head sink nicely into the bed or pillow under you.

Feel your arms relaxing.

Yours legs relaxing, even the muscles around your head and face softening and relaxing.

If you need to, wiggle around a little bit, so you are comfortable.

Snuggle up in your soft blankets, and hug your stuffed toy, if you have one.

Gently close your eyes.

Nothing else to do now except relax, listening to my voice.

As your body and mind get ready for a restful soothing sleep, let's begin our story – *School Days Ahead*!

It is only a few days before a new school year will begin. And Sonali, Deco and Pariya have lots to say on their feelings about the coming days. This is going to be Deco and Pariya's first year of grade school, and they are feeling a little anxious about what to expect in grade one. They know it will be different from daycare, and not at all like staying home all day.

Deco and Pariya are talking to each other in the playground this late summer day – wondering what the first days of school will be like. Sonali is really excited about going to school in grade three. They could not understand why Sonali was so thrilled about school.

Deco told Pariya he always had fun at daycare and liked his friends there.

And, the summer camp days were also loaded with fun activities like crafts, bicycle rides, and exploring walks to the nearby forest park. Deco told Pariya that grade one seemed to be more work, than daycare play. He remembers the homework that his sister Sonali brought home. She always liked doing homework.

Yet Deco was worried he couldn't read as well as his older sister. And he wondered, "Would there still be time to play after school days?"
Pariya told Deco she also feels troubled about starting grade one. Like Deco, she had fun friends at daycare, and she was worried they may not go to the same grade one classroom as her. Pariya also felt she might miss her favourite friend in the whole world – her sister Elika. Elika is still too young to go to school, so she will be at home or daycare when Pariya is in grade one.

Sonali was also at the playground and overheard some of what Pariya and Deco were wondering about the beginning of a new school year. Sonali has already completed grades one and two. She really wants to get back together with old school friends – and to meet new friends in grade three.

She told Deco and Pariya that she was also anxious about going to school at first, before Grade One – but that she had talked about her feelings with her parents. Talking to adults about your worries can be very helpful.

Sonali reassured Pariya and Deco that there is a chance some of the daycare friends will also be at the same school in grade one. There is an even stronger chance that they would make new friends in grade one.

And like the wise eight-year-old she is, Sonali also suggested that there are a bunch of ways to have fun with new and old friends as they begin school. She mentioned that the classroom is only one place to meet new friends. There is also 'recess'. Recess is a break from classwork learning and is usually outside in a play area. It is a good time to meet new friends and play games. Deco thought about that and told Pariya and Sonali he loves outside playtime and that he made friends in the playground at daycare. He's liking recess already!

Then Sonali pointed out that the walk or school bus trip to school also offers a chance to meet new friends. So does lunchtime! And sometimes there are even after-school opportunities to play. And, speaking of plays, Sonali told them how each class also plans one or two school plays or presentations each school year. Everyone in the classroom works together as a team to put on a show for the parents, like Christmas plays in December. It might be a play where some classmates speak, some sing, others dance. And it is a lot of fun.

Deco smiled happily. He remembered a play when Sonali sang in grade two. He remembered the hand-drawn and coloured decorations made by Sonali and her classmates. He couldn't wait to put his drawing skills to work on his first play in grade one!

That's when Pariya shouted out "Yay!". She loves singing and dancing and knows some of her classmates will like it too. And now she was looking forward to lunchtime too. In daycare, she had a lot of good lunchtime chats with others in her class – and with her teachers too.

Deco also remembered that Sonali missed him when she was at school all day. But that they would catch up and have lots of fun during the evenings and weekends. That made Pariya feel much better about Elika staying at home or daycare while she went to school. She always liked the big, long, hugs with her sister when they got together again.

As Deco and Pariya thought about school now, they liked thinking about the exciting days ahead. New friends, lots of activities, playtime at recess and of course, learning in the classroom too.

Deco suddenly looked a little more concerned. A slight frown appeared on his face for a moment. Sonali noticed. She asked, "What is wrong?"

Deco told her he doesn't know how to read like her. He knows a few words, but not full storybooks like Sonali. That's when Sonali reminded him that she also could not read full storybooks either, when she began grade one. She learned how to read more, in school, and by doing her homework. She looked at Pariya and Deco and promised them they will learn how to read, to write, just like her, in school.

Sonali told them she is looking forward to reading more books and learning to write even more stories – something she enjoys doing at home, even during the summer months off school. She promised them that they too would learn everything they need in school, but she also promised to help them, if they need help at anytime.

Then Pariya also spoke up about helping others. She says talking to her parents about anything that bothered her at daycare was always helpful to her. Parents can provide understanding that young people may not have even thought about. She remembered her parents asking what the best thing was about her day at daycare, and they would ask if anything was wrong if she seemed sad that day.

Sonali agreed that talking to parents is a good idea. She also told them that parents often get them prepared for school, by starting bedtime "routines" a few days before school begins. A routine might mean the same time waking up and going to bed each night and always getting clothes ready for the next day. She said some parents, even before the first day of school, bring their kids to visit the new school, and sometimes, to meet their new teacher.

Now, Deco and Pariya are really feeling a lot of support from Sonali. And they know they will have a lot of help from Mom and Dad. They're feeling excited about beginning school in a few days; Meeting new friends, new teachers, new experiences!

Leaving the playground for the short walk back home, Sonali, Deco and Pariya are now feeling ready for school days ahead, and all the fun it will bring to each of them – and to their new friends.
At the end of this day, they are now ready for a restful sleep. You too, can slip into sleep, anytime.

Gently close your eyes.
You are safe here.

Let's take a big deep breath to help us relax into sleepytime.
Take a deep breath in - filling your whole body with all that good energy….
Then let out all that old air – long breath out…

Now, let all thoughts of the day, or of school days, float far, far, away.

If you wish, take those deep breaths in and out one or two more times, and then, just breathe naturally.

You may keep noticing your breath. With every breath out, you feel more and more relaxed.

More ready, for a restful, deep, sleep.

It is time now, for pleasant and sweet dreams.

The Fearsome Four and the Yellow Pumpkin

Welcome to a story about *the Fearsome Four and the Yellow Pumpkin*.
Before we head out to the pumpkin patch, let's get settled for a relaxing and restful bedtime story.

Cozy up now, into those soft cuddly blankets, and a snugly toy, if you have one.

Let's get comfy.

Lay down in your bed, on your back, if that makes you feel ready and calm.

Think about making your body relaxed.

If you need to, wiggle around a bit to settle in.

Gently close your eyes.

You are safe here.

Now, notice your breathing.

Thinking about your breathing helps you relax.

Let's take three long deep breaths.

A deep breath in…

And, then a slow, long, breath out….

Again… deep breath in…

And, then a slow, long, breath out….

Very good! One more time.

Deep breath in…

And, then a slow, long, breath out….

Eyes closed.

Calmly breathing.

One day in the pumpkin patch, where the field was dotted with hundreds of bright orange pumpkins, there was one little spec in the field, that didn't look the same as the others. It was a pumpkin, but it was yellow, not orange. It was yellow, even though it had grown in the same way, same place, and same conditions, like sun and water – as the others. But Yellow Pumpkin, just knew it was not like the others.

Some of the other pumpkins were not sure what to think of Yellow Pumpkin, being so different from them. So, it seemed that Yellow Pumpkin was rarely invited into their conversations, or to their games. That made Yellow Pumpkin sad. Left out. And feeling alone.

That day, a group of children known as the Fearsome Four, traveled to the pumpkin farm, to choose a pumpkin to bring home, for Halloween.

Sonali was the oldest of the group, so she often led the way for the four. Though the others each could take the lead when they wanted to. Sonali's intention was to get a huge orange pumpkin, and the others, Deco, Pariya and Elika thought that was a good idea. However, they each wanted to see if they could find the perfect pumpkin.

The Fearsome Four set out on a mission, splitting up, and wandering throughout the pumpkin patch in all directions – searching for the perfect, big, orange, pumpkin.

After a few minutes, Deco called out to the others. He had found a tall and slim orange pumpkin. That was a good possibility, as it stood out taller than most of the other pumpkins. It might be the tallest one in their neighborhood, when all the houses on the street have pumpkins and other Halloween decorations on display. Maybe this one, Deco thought.

Then, Pariya discovered another good possible choice – a very round pumpkin that was large enough that it would take all four of them to carry it home. It would surely be the largest one on display on their street. Now they had two great possibilities, and at first, they were very content with having to decide between only two.

Then Sonali shouted out to the others from one side of the patch – She had found a third possibility – a very wide, and very short, orange, pumpkin. It was kind of cute, and she thought a really wide smile could be carved out of this one – for the biggest smile in the neighborhood.

Sonali, Deco and Pariya gathered, to talk about the three possible pumpkins. Would they choose one of these to take home? They would each have one vote for the choice, and then come to an agreement. But, there should be four in the Fearsome Four – not three! They looked around, for Elika. She should join in the decision, too. But where was Elika?

With their eyes, the three scanned the entire area; looking north, looking south, looking east and looking west, and there was no sign, of Elika. Three of the Fearsome Four began to worry, just a little. Where did she go? Could they find her?

For a whole minute, they walked up and down the paths of the pumpkin field, jumping over some of the big green leaves of the pumpkin plants. Those leaves are very important to the plant's growth – they capture energy from the sun to help the pumpkin grow larger, and the leaves also provide shade, protecting the big orange fruit from getting too much sun. Most people never see those large leaves because we buy the pumpkins at the store, long after the leaves are gone. Maybe Elika was somewhere under one of those leaves?

The search continued, and just then, Sonali saw some of those leaves moving, over the far south end of the field. As they ran closer, they could see Elika was squatting down, sheltered somewhat by those big green leaves, and she was looking at an unusual, and very different, pumpkin.

There was Yellow Pumpkin, which didn't look like all the others. Yellow Pumpkin worried the Fearsome Four would reject it – because it wasn't the nice bright orange colour that they had expected to find at the pumpkin patch that day.

Yet, something special happened in the moments that followed.

Elika had come to realize that every one of the Fearsome Four, were also different from the others, in some way. For example, Sonali liked reading books, Deco liked fishing, Pariya liked skating, and Elika was especially fond of dancing. She knew that they loved each other – and often because of those differences! Each of their choices made them different. And, they were all beautiful, in their very own way.

They knew there was only one Pariya, only one Deco, only one Sonali and only one Elika – in the whole world.

They knew they were each special – that being a little different from the others is not only OK – but even made everything more interesting and more enjoyable. Together they thought, "Wouldn't the days be so boring if everyone was exactly the same? If they always wanted the same thing?

Much of the fun the Fearsome Four had, whenever they played together, was because they each saw the world in a slightly unique way. That meant they each could dream up new and fun games and activities to play – with fresh ideas that the other three had not considered. In being different, even one of a kind – there was strength. There are more ways to have fun than any one mind or mindset could imagine. If there was a problem to solve, the Fearsome Four together could solve it.

As Sonali, Deco, Pariya and Elika talked about this in front of Yellow Pumpkin, it began to feel much better about being different. Being a little different from others is a good thing after all.

Yellow Pumpkin now felt more valued, and much happier with this sense of being accepted just the way it is. The Fearsome Four had now quickly come to a conclusion. This year was the year of the Yellow Pumpkin. Yellow Pumpkin was coming home.

And, as the day turned into early evening, Yellow Pumpkin was decorated, beautifully carved to have a happy face, and was ready for Halloween. People walking along the street would stop and talk about how super special that yellow pumpkin was. They said, it was nice to see one that was unlike all the others.

Yellow Pumpkin was proud. The Fearsome Four had made its day!

As the sunset arrived at the end of this long, beautiful day exploring the pumpkin patch, each of the Fearsome Four were now snuggled into their beds, yawning, and ready for a deep, restful, sleep.

Let's also prepare for sleep now.
Eyes are closed.

You are breathing…. slowly… and calmly…
Notice your breathing as you settle in for a night of deep, deep, sleep.
With each breath inward, you feel calmer and calmer, and your mind is ready for rest too.
Nothing else to do. Nothing else to think about.
Your body is feeling heavier, and heavier, and gently supported by the bed under you.
You feel relaxed now.
You are comfy.
Cozy.
Safe.

It is time now… for pleasant, and sweet dreams.

A Not So Spooky Story

Welcome to a not-so-spooky bedtime story. Prepare not to be spooked as Boris and his older brother Boo Boo get ready for an enchanted adventure.

Before I read this boo-tiful story to you, let's protect you from any spine-tingling chills.

Cozy up now, into those soft cuddly blankets, and a snugly toy creature, if you have one.

No need to be afraid. It's just a bedtime story; a not-so-spooky, spooky story! Let's get comfy.

Lay down in your bed, on your back, if that makes you comfortable.

Think about making your body calm, relaxed. Wiggle around a bit, if you need to.

You are safe here.

Notice your breathing. Thinking about your breathing - each breath in… and each breath out… helps you to relax.

Now, gently close your eyes.

Calmly breathing.

It is time for our not-so-spooky story!

Boris and his older brother, Boo Boo, knew that Halloween was still many days away, and so it was time to get prepared for the things that happen on that spookiest night of the year. They know that the things they will do to get ready, don't need to wait until Halloween. Most things they wanted to do, could happen anytime one wants to have some spooktacular fun.

Boo Boo remembers last Halloween, when he gathered many treats from friends and family in the neighbourhood. He doesn't remember saying "trick or treat" all the time, but he does remember smiles whenever he said "thank you" for getting a treat.

He also remembers people really liking his costume, and the fun he had making the costume. Boo Boo was dressed as a spooky ghost. Boris had helped him craft the ghost outfit from an old white cloth pillowcase that mom gave him. They had cut holes in the top and sides for Boo Boo's head, and his arms. And marked the white pillowcase with some black charcoal lines – to make it appear more scary. Boo Boo also had white powdery make-up on his face, and black make-up around his eyes to look like a ghost, though Boo Boo liked smiling so much – so he was surely a friendly ghost.

This time, Boo Boo wanted Boris to help him make another costume – this time Boo Boo wanted to dress up as a big orange pumpkin. Boris was afraid of spiders, yet he still had a collection of small plastic spiders to play with. So, he suggested putting a big black spider and even a spider web, on the pumpkin costume. Boo Boo thought that was a great idea, but they wondered, "What would they need to make the big orange pumpkin costume?"

Together, they thought about it. Then, Boo Boo remembered that their Dad had a large orange tee-shirt that he used to wear all the time. Now it was too old and worn, and it might be in a box of old clothing their parents used for things like painting walls and ceilings. Maybe they could find that tee shirt and turn it into a pumpkin costume. The box would probably be in storage, in the basement.

As they walked down the creaky stairs, they left the daylight behind, and slowly walked down into the dark, gloomy, shadows, of the basement. Boo Boo didn't like going to the basement. It was darker there than elsewhere in their home. And, the basement smelled odd. Maybe it was the scent of creatures hiding there – or maybe it was just the musty smell of dampness and old things that sometimes make basements smell that way.

Boris didn't like going to the basement either – as he knew that spiders like to spin their sticky webs in dark and damp places, like basements. He would be careful. Very careful!

In the basement, there were a lot of storage boxes, old bicycle parts, Dad's tools, and old camping gear. One box in the corner looked like it had something draped across it, like a very thin blanket. As they stepped nearer though – Boris stopped in his tracks, with fear. That wasn't a blanket — It was a huge spider web! Boris told Boo Boo HE wasn't going to check THAT box!

They couldn't see the spider that made the big web. Maybe it has been gone a long time. Or maybe, it is still hiding, nearby. Boris wasn't going to take any chances. He stayed as far as he could from that spider web – on the other side of the basement room!

As Boris stepped backward — away from the spider web — he was not paying attention to where he was going, and his back bumped into the stuff behind him.

Oops! He bumped into a shelf holding a bunch of sports equipment, and suddenly, it was tumbling off the shelf down to Boris and Boo Boo. It was like they were under attack by a mysterious creature, as soccer balls, volleyballs, and basketballs rained down onto them. They were not hurt, but they were surprised!

As they began picking up the balls to return to the shelf, Boo Boo noticed an old cardboard box with paint stains on it. That might be the box with the orange tee-shirt!

The top of the box was dusty. And the dim light in the basement room looked smoky as they brushed the dust off the top of the box. Boris asked Boo Boo to open the box – He was afraid a spider, might be lurking just under the cover. As Boo Boo nervously pulled the top of the box open, they were surprised again. But, this time, it wasn't a spooky surprise. It was a pleasant one.

There it was. The orange tee shirt sitting right on the top of the pile of folded clothes in the box. Boris was also pleased. He really wanted to get out of there!

Just then, there came a rumbling, almost growling sound, from the other side of the basement, in the next room. They thought about running out of there before they would see whatever may be prowling behind the door in the next room. But Boo Boo was too curious. He just had to know what it was!

He approached the door, and slowly creaked it open. Again, the dull, rumbling noise. What could it be? They had to turn on the light switch, to find out.

Boris wasn't sure about this. So, he stood behind Boo Boo as he flicked the light switch – and at that moment there was a big whoosh sound — Oh, it's just the furnace starting up to warm up the house. Boo Boo had forgotten about the sounds the furnace makes when the days get colder, near Halloween. Now, knowing their discovery was nothing to be afraid of, Boris and Boo Boo had a laugh, and started their way back upstairs, with the orange tee shirt in hand.

That afternoon, they worked on drawing lines on the tee shirt, to make it look like a bright and happy pumpkin, and they would tie up the bottom of the tee shirt slightly and stuff it with crinkled paper to fill out the pumpkin so it would look big and round on Boo Boo.

Boris went to pick out one of his favourite black plastic spiders from his collection, and they glued some strings to the costume to make the spider's web.
Boo Boo's costume was ready!

As all this was happening, Boo Boo's mom was in the kitchen, baking, and now a not so spooky smell was in the air. She was baking a fresh pumpkin pie for after dinner.

After a busy and exciting day, Boris and Boo Boo feasted on dinner – and dessert – the delicious still-warm pumpkin pie.

They were now ready for Halloween, and after all this activity, ready for their story time and sleep.

Let's also get set for sleep. You are ready, for a very restful night of sleep. Eyes are closed.
You are breathing…. slowly… and calmly…
Continue watching your breathing - each breath in… and each breath out… as you settle in, for a night of deep, deep, sleep.

Let your body feel more and more relaxed.
Your body and bones on this not so spooky night, sinking softly into the bed under you.
Nothing else to do. Nothing else to think about.

You are comfy.
Cozy.
Safe.

It is time now… for pleasant, and sweet dreams.

Acknowledgments

The author is grateful for background music (audiobook) and images by various artists as follows:

Images/Photos:
Several of the photos and other images in this book were created by the author. Drawing of the Angry Flower is by the author's granddaughter Sonali, and the hollow log star by an artist friend Cyrille Deveau. In addition, the following images were provided by these contributors on Pixabay, (including the lovely image used on the book cover and end of each story, by Prawny):

Prawny, bookwurmee, Maky_Orel, OpenClipart-Vectors, Lara_Yin, Hugo_Ob, Clker-Free-Vector-Images, blickpixel, geralt, milaoktasafitri, tanrıca, Syeda Saira, Mystic Art Design, Hansuan_Fabregas, Michelle_Pitzel, Baptiste Lheurette, Blender Timer, GDJ, Lolame, PublicDomainPictures, Pexels, Dimitris Vetsika, 99mimimi.

Audiobook:
Background music for each chapter was provided by these Pixabay contributors:

The Angry Flower - Lullaby Music Vol. 8 by Piotr Witowski.
Thank Your Lucky Stars - Sleep Music Vol. 17 by Relaxing Time.
Legend of the Fireflies - Quiet Contemplation Meditation 283536 by

NaturesEye.

Secret Superpowers in my Sleep - Lullaby Music Vol. 8 by Piotr Witowski.

The Best Presents Ever - Sweet Dreams by RelaxingTime.

Picnic Mountain and the Leaning Bench - Mountain Hike by Alex Wit Light_Music.

Exploring the Ocean - Dreaming Seas by NaturesEye.

Exploring the Universe - Lost in Space – Ambient Soundscape by NaturesEye.

Exploring the Forest - Nature Walk by Olexy.

School Days Ahead - Sleep Music Vol. 15 by Relaxing Time Piotr Witowski.

The Fearsome Four and the Yellow Pumpkin - Lullaby Music by Piotr Witowski.

A Not so Spooky Story - Meditation 3 +432Hz +768 Hz by TwinFishAudio.

About the Author

Andy LeBlanc is a lifelong storyteller who infuses every tale with calm, curiosity, and wisdom. Guided by the candid insights of his four grandchildren, he crafts soothing narrations that weave meaningful lessons into engaging tales. His stories are designed to relax, inspire, and create lasting connections with children of all ages.

Visit FocusSpede.ca or send comments to the author at Andy@FocusSpede.ca

You can connect with me on:

🌐 http://focusspede.ca